Apply within!

The Best (& Worst) Jobs in
ANCIENT EGYPT

Clive Gifford

WAYLAND

First published in Great Britain in 2015 by Wayland

Copyright © Wayland, 2015

Editor: Nicola Edwards

Designer: Rocket Design (East Anglia) Ltd

Illustrations by Alex Paterson

Dewey number: 331.7'00932–dc23

ISBN: 978 0 7502 8736 4

Library eBook ISBN: 978 0 7502 8743 2

10 9 8 7 6 5 4 3 2 1

Wayland, an imprint of

Hachette Children's Group

Part of Hodder and Stoughton

Carmelite House

50 Victoria Embankment

London EC4Y 0DZ

An Hachette UK Company

www.hachette.co.uk

www.hachettechildrens.co.uk

Printed and bound in China

All photographs supplied by
The Art Archive (www.art-archive.com)
except for pp 5 (both), and p23
(bottom left) Shutterstock.com

CONTENTS

THE JOB MARKET
IN ANCIENT EGYPT

So you're looking for employment in ancient Egypt? Good on you!

It's a growing job market ever since two separate kingdoms, Upper Egypt and Lower Egypt, united in about 3100 BCE. The ancient Egyptian civilization would be incredibly long-running, lasting almost 3,000 years. During that time, the ancient Egyptians made great advances in science, the arts, medicine, learning and government. They developed surveying and construction techniques to build large cities, giant temples and extraordinary burial tombs for their rulers.

Mediterranean Sea

• Alexandria

LOWER EGYPT

Giza •

Memphis • • (Cairo)

SINAI

River Nile

Red Sea

UPPER EGYPT

Valley of the Kings

• Thebes

Lake Nasser

• (Aswan)

ODD JOB

GOOD GRIEF!

Not everyone was a farmer, builder or pharaoh. Some ancient Egyptians were professional mourners. They were paid to be upset from when a person died to when they were buried — sometimes a period of 70 days — during which they would cry, wail and throw dust over themselves!

Running 6,600 km south to north before emptying into the Mediterranean Sea, the mighty River Nile was ancient Egypt's life-source, providing water for drinking and farming as well as providing a vital transport and trade link for boats.

The Great Pyramid was built just over 4,500 years ago during the reign of Pharaoh Khufu. At 146 m high, it was the world's tallest building for more than 3,800 years.

As an ancient Egyptian, whatever job you did, you would have to endure the region's hot, dry climate as well as a ten-day working week. Holidays were few and you would often have to spend them taking part in religious ceremonies, praying and giving offerings to the gods. The rulers of ancient Egypt, the pharaohs, were also treated like living gods and their orders had to be obeyed at all costs. To see what jobs were on offer in ancient Egypt and which were the best and worst, read on…

The majestic Temple of Karnak was an enormous temple complex. One of its buildings, the Hypostyle Hall, was almost the size of a football pitch and featured 134 giant columns, many 24 m high.

ODD JOB

MULTITASKING

Many ancient Egyptians held down more than one job. For example, some soldiers during peacetime became policemen and even used the world's first police sniffer dogs to track down criminals.

FARMER

Seasonal work

Most farmers worked lands close to the River Nile. Their year was divided into three seasons: flooding (*Akhet*), growing (*Peret*) and harvesting (*Shemu*). Each year around June, the Nile flooded, depositing rich, fertile silt on the farmlands. During this period, farmers had to watch out as the pharaoh or nobles sometimes forced them to leave their land and labour on a big building project such as a pyramid or temple. This was known as *corvee* or labour tax. The growing season began after the floods receded in October or November.

Farmers in ancient Egypt broke up the soil using a wooden plough pulled by cattle. Seeds were sown by hand and trodden into the soil.

Keep going, keep growing

Farmers worked long, hard hours, tending, watering and weeding their crops. These included wheat, barley and flax (which was spun into linen cloth) as well as vegetables such as beans, onions and cucumbers. Farmers also had to look after animals including cattle, goats and geese.

Cereal crops were harvested in early ancient Egypt using a wooden sickle fitted with sharpened teeth made of flint. By the time of the Middle Kingdom, sharp sickles made of bronze were used.

In addition to farm work, farmers had to find time to pray and make offerings to gods such as the harvest goddess, Renenutet. At harvest time from March to May everyone in a farmer's family pitched in to gather all the crops. While some of the crop would be given as an offering to gods, the pharaoh's officials forced farmers to give up an additional 10 per cent or more of it as a tax.

WORK MATES

When the Nile flooded, boundaries marked between the fields of different farmers were often washed away. This led to disputes. Rope stretchers were officials armed with 12m-long ropes, knotted every cubit (about 52cm), who measured out and re-marked the field boundaries.

JOB VERDICT

Hard, back-breaking work with few holidays but plenty to eat (if the harvests were good).

EMBALMER

No-brainer

The mummy-making process took 70 days and had several stages. First, the embalmers took out the brain by chiselling into the skull through the nose and pulling it out bit-by-bit. Then they removed the internal organs, the liver, stomach, lungs and guts from the body. After that they covered the body with natron, a type of salt, to dry it out.

JOB VACANCY
Start date: 1500 BCE

- ARE YOU FAMED THROUGHOUT THE MIDDLE EAST FOR YOUR SKILL AND KNOWLEDGE?
- DO YOU KNOW HOW TO USE PRAYERS, SPELLS AND MAGIC CHARMS?
- CAN YOU PULL OUT A BRAIN THROUGH THE NOSE OF A DEAD BODY?

A tomb painting (below left) shows an embalmer at work. The dead body was placed on a table (left) and a sharp flint knife was used to cut into the body.

ODD JOB

PET PRESERVING

It wasn't only people that were embalmed. Ancient Egyptians often made mummies out of their dead pets or of creatures used as offerings to their gods. Around half a million mummified ibis birds were made as offerings to Thoth, the god of wisdom, at the burial ground of Saqqara alone!

Well preserved

After about 40 days, when the body was completely dry, embalmers stuffed it with linen soaked in oil and resin, a sticky liquid from plants, and stitched it up. They rubbed palm oil into the skin to soften it, and sometimes even stuffed mud or animal fat into cuts in the body as padding. Finally, to create a mummy, the embalmers wrapped the body in layers of bandages, with a total length of up to 1.6 km. This was then placed in a decorated wooden coffin, often finished with a portrait of the dead person on its lid.

Embalmers used these painted wooden jars to store the brains and internal organs they removed from dead bodies.

JOB VERDICT

With high status and good working conditions, this is one of the best – if you've got the guts to handle guts!

SOLDIER

A soldier's life

Life as a foot soldier could be hard, with long exhausting marches across hot lands and bloodthirsty battles with hand-to-hand combat and a real risk of death. During peacetime, soldiers might be set to work as labourers, building irrigation canals or a new temple on the pharaoh's orders. Beatings were common punishments for any soldier who stepped out of line. You would carry a weapon such as a spear, short sword, a club or axe but you'd have no armour to protect you. At best, you might carry a small wooden shield, covered in leather. Soldiers were fed and housed by the army but had to carry their own food while they were on the move.

Arrowing in

Within the army there were different career options. A fierce, experienced soldier might be promoted to become a standard bearer in charge of 200 regular soldiers. One who was strong and had good eyesight might become an archer. These lucky soldiers started battles a good 100-200 m away from the enemy, firing sharp arrows.

This copy of a tomb painting shows a group of ancient Egyptian soldiers marching forward. The soldier on the far right is the standard bearer.

THAT'S HANDY!

In victory, soldiers were often rewarded with slaves, gold or other valuables for the number of enemy they had killed. Under some commanders, soldiers had to cut off the hands or even the penises of their victims to show their success in battle.

This stone relief from the temple of Ramesses III shows an archer. Archers used compound bows made of many layers of wood, animal sinew and horn.

JOB VERDICT

Tough, brutal and poorly paid – unless you were often on the winning side, as then you could receive riches plundered from your defeated enemies.

PHARAOH

A God on Earth

In ancient Egypt, the pharaohs or kings had complete control of the country's wealth, could make new laws and build new cities, majestic temples and other buildings to honour themselves and the gods. Their every need was looked after by a large collection of servants and they left most of the day-to-day running of the country to their advisors. As a pharaoh you would wear the finest linen clothes and jewels, you'd be complimented at every occasion, treated like the ultimate celebrity and feast at evening banquets entertained by dancers and musicians as well as enjoying afternoons cruising down the Nile.

Responsibilities

It wasn't all fun, fun, fun. You would have many advisors, wives and children to deal with. Just remembering all their names could be a chore for a pharaoh like Ramesses II who is said to have had eight wives, 96 sons and 60 daughters!

JOB VACANCY
Start date: 1500 BCE

- ARE YOU THE PHARAOH'S ELDEST SON?
- COULD YOU BEHAVE AS THOUGH YOU WERE A GOD ON EARTH?
- WOULD YOU ENJOY RECEIVING COMPLIMENTS ALL DAY, EVERY DAY?
- CAN YOU MAKE BIG DECISIONS ABOUT WHICH WARS TO FIGHT AND WHO TO TRADE WITH?

NOTE: ORDINARY EGYPTIANS NEED NOT APPLY.

The funerary mask of the pharaoh Tutankhamun is made from solid gold. Buried in his tomb with him were over 5,300 of his possessions including chariots, sandals covered in gold leaf and leopard skin cloaks.

To protect Egypt, some kings led from the front during military campaigns. Pharaoh Katmose died in battle, and Thutmose II was nearly trampled to death by elephants in Syria. Some pharaohs had to watch their backs at home. Ramesses III, for example, was murdered by having his throat cut. And if you did survive and ruled for 30 years (and every three years after that), you would have to prove your fitness to govern by running or performing other physical tasks at the Heb-Sed festival.

The pharaoh Ramesses wears a blue crown and holds the hair of three prisoners in this painted stone block which is more than 3,200 years old.

ODD JOB

FEMALE PHARAOH

Nearly all pharaohs were men, but Queen Hatshepsut ruled Egypt from 1478 BCE for just over 20 years. She sent expeditions to other parts of Africa and ordered hundreds of new buildings to be built — and wore a false beard on her chin.

JOB VERDICT

The top, top job in ancient Egypt. Unlimited power, riches and glory – but watch out for any plots to topple you.

SLAVE

Owned at home

Ancient Egypt relied on slaves less than many other ancient civilizations. Most of the slaves in ancient Egypt were foreign prisoners of war. However, some were Egyptians living in poverty who sold their children or themselves into slavery or were sold by foreign slave traders. Archaeologists have found records of the pharaoh, Amenhotep III ordering 40 slave girls for 40 kit (about 360 g) of silver per girl. Once owned, slaves could not regain their freedom unless their owner granted it. Some slaves were even tattooed with marks of ownership.

JOB VACANCY
Start date: 1500 BCE

* HAVE YOU BEEN CAPTURED IN BATTLE?
* WAS YOUR FAMILY SO POOR THAT THEY HAD TO SELL YOU?
* ARE YOU NOT LOOKING FOR CAREER ADVANCEMENT?
* WOULD YOU BE PREPARED TO BE THE LOWEST OF THE LOW IN EGYPTIAN SOCIETY?

Lucky or unlucky

As a slave you didn't get to choose the work you did, it was chosen for you. Some slaves got a lucky break and worked indoors cooking and cleaning. Others were less lucky. They might be put to work grinding cereal crops into flour, carrying water from the Nile to distant farm fields or other menial tasks that others preferred

This painting from the tomb of a scribe shows a slave being beaten to the floor by his master (right) while another slave begs for mercy.

not to do. Some of the unluckiest slaves worked in terrible conditions in hot, cramped copper and gold mines in the desert. With no safety measures in place and water strictly rationed, many slave miners perished due to the intense heat, rock falls or dehydration, a lack of water.

A female slave grinds cereal grain into flour. Female slaves performed many jobs around the homes of wealthy Egyptians. Slaves could be inherited by an owner's son or daughter.

ODD JOB

SWEET DEAL

Pharaoh Pepi II is said to have kept a couple of slaves covered head to toe in honey. Sounds delicious but it was so they would attract flies and other insects, some of which could bite and sting, to keep them away from the king.

JOB VERDICT

It all depends. Job satisfaction could vary, from relatively high for a trusted slave given interesting work by a kind owner to very low for those working for a brutal and unforgiving master.

SCRIBE

Scribe school

To become a scribe took many years of schooling, often starting at the age of eight or nine. Only the sons of scribes were guaranteed a place, although some sons of wealthier families were also admitted. Over many years, students learned more than 700 different symbols that made up the hieroglyphic writing system as well as another writing system called hieratic. They practised their writing on stones and broken pottery pieces known as ostraca. Students were fearful of getting a symbol wrong as their mistakes were often punished with a painful whack from the teacher's stick.

JOB VACANCY
Start date: 1500 BCE

- ARE YOU A GOOD STUDENT, TERRIFIC AT READING AND WRITING?
- DO YOU HAVE LOTS OF PATIENCE AND A GOOD MEMORY?
- DOES THE IDEA OF HELPING TO RUN THE MIGHTY EGYPTIAN EMPIRE APPEAL TO YOU?
- ARE YOU AMBITIOUS WITH A DESIRE TO MOVE UP IN THE WORLD?

NOTE: GIRLS NEED NOT APPLY.

Written work

Fewer than one in a hundred ancient Egyptians could read or write, so scribes were always in demand and had high status in society. Some scribes were available for hire in cities while

A scribe's tools of his trade included pens made of frayed reeds, which were dipped in ink mixed in the ink well of a palette made of stone or wood. Scribes wrote on papyrus scrolls made of the stripped and flattened fibres of papyrus reeds.

others with a thirst for adventure travelled with armies to write reports and order supplies. Scribes were vital in keeping Egypt's government running smoothly. They were employed to draw up contracts and write letters, collect taxes and record all sorts of important information from details of harvests to conducting censuses of the population.

A scribe sits cross-legged so that he can work on a papyrus sheet or tablet.

A scribe (top centre) records the numbers of seated prisoners in this stone carving from the tomb of Horemheb, the scribe who became pharaoh (see below).

ODD JOB

FRINGE BENEFITS

Some scribes rose through the ranks to become advisors to nobles or even the pharaoh. One scribe, Horemheb, managed to go further, becoming pharaoh in c.1319 BCE and ruling Egypt for more than 25 years.

JOB VERDICT

No heavy lifting, no need to join the army and no taxes, what's there not to like? Being a scribe was high status work, with the chance to move up into the higher ranks of society. Great job!

17

FISHERMAN

Hooked in

The River Nile was full of fish and some poorer people fished from its banks to supplement their diets. These occasional fishermen used spears or curved, J-shaped hooks with a barb on their point, similar to those still used today. Ancient Egyptian hooks were made of copper or bronze and cast out on a handheld line made of flax or linen. Full-time fishermen used multiple hooks on the same line or invested what little wealth and spare time they had on large nets made of knotted cords which had to be repaired regularly.

This limestone relief shows a fisherman pulling a weighted drag net along the river bed.

WORK MATES

Other Nile workers included ferrymen who carried people and goods from one bank of the Nile to the other, and washermen. Being a washerman was one of the grimmest jobs in ancient Egypt, scrubbing other people's sweaty, dirty loin cloths in the waters of the Nile. Apart from being unpleasant work, it could also be seriously dangerous as lurking close to the river bank were often crocodiles and hippos keen to attack.

These 4000-year-old models show how fishermen would sometimes work together, suspending a drift net between their two papyrus reed boats to gather in as many fish from the middle of the river as they could.

A fishy business

You would need to know your different species of fish. Some, like carp, mullet or eels were tasty and prized. Others, such as the garmout, tasted foul, had poisonous spines, or in the case of the electric catfish, gave off a surprisingly sharp electric shock. Ouch!

Once caught, fish were either gutted then dried in the sun and salted to preserve them, or taken to market. Fishermen could often trade their catch for other food from bakers, farmers and other market traders. After a day's fishing and trading under the hot sun, boy would you stink, but hopefully, you could go home happy to your family who may wear fish-shaped lucky charms called amulets to protect you from drowning.

JOB VERDICT

Not bad as long as you managed to gather a good catch regularly and avoid the attentions of hippos and crocodiles. Your poor family, though, would have to get used to you smelling of fish!

PRIEST

Religion was a major part of everyday life in ancient Egypt so priests were highly respected. Some, known as wab or lector priests, were part-time, and worked in their normal jobs for most of the year. Others were priests all year round, tending the temple, giving prayers, taking part in funeral ceremonies or religious holidays and performing tasks for the temple chief, the head priest. Each temple had its own rules and rituals. Priests weren't allowed to eat fish or wear wool, for example, while at many temples, they would bathe in sacred pools three or four times a day to cleanse themselves.

JOB VACANCY
Start date: 1500 BCE

- ARE YOU PREPARED TO DEVOTE YOUR LIFE TO THE ANCIENT EGYPTIAN GODS?
- ARE YOU OKAY WITH NOT EATING FISH OR WEARING WOOL?
- DO YOU LIKE BATHS?

This painting on papyrus shows a priest making an offering to the gods in the temple.

JOB VERDICT

A bit dull with all those prayers and rituals but otherwise pretty good. Landing a job as a priest at a major temple could be difficult though, as the positions were often filled by members of the pharaoh's or local nomarch's family (see page 25).

DOCTOR

As ancient Egypt progressed, medicine grew from folk healing with chants and prayers into something much closer to science. You'd mix religion with remedies as an ancient Egyptian doctor. You might offer prayers and amulets to ward off evil spirits but you would also be able to set broken bones, perform simple surgery and seal wounds with a hot knife and then cover them with honey to stop infection. You would have a good knowledge of herbs as you would make a large range of your own remedies. You might crush aloe vera leaves and cucumber in wine, for example, to make a lotion to cure skin complaints.

JOB VACANCY
Start date: 1500 BCE

- ARE YOU GOOD WITH GORE – AND DON'T MIND PATIENTS SCREAMING?
- HAVE YOU SPENT MANY MONTHS READING ANCIENT TEMPLE SCROLLS TO KNOW ALL ABOUT MEDICINE?
- DO YOU KNOW YOUR CUMIN FROM YOUR JUNIPER AND PLENTY OF OTHER PLANTS BESIDES?

ODD JOB
REVOLTING REMEDIES

One ancient Egyptian remedy to cure baldness required the fat of a lion and a hippo, gazelle dung and spit...Urgh! There's worse... A remedy for eye complaints from the Ebers Papyrus suggests mixing dead human brain with honey before smearing it over the eye... Double Urgh!

JOB VERDICT

Prospects are good, and as a doctor you'd gain high status in society if enough of your patients were happy with your treatments and lived to recommend you to others!

BUILDER

Muddy matters

Most ordinary buildings in ancient Egypt were constructed out of mud bricks. The material proved a good insulator to keep heat out but it wasn't long-lasting, and so people had to rebuild every few years. This provided a steady stream of work for brick makers, labourers and bricklayers, all of whom had to toil hard to make a living especially as it took an estimated 4-5,000 bricks to build a small Egyptian house. Brick makers would go home covered in caked-on mud which could smell foul in the heat of summer.

The mud mixture would be pressed into wooden moulds like this and left to dry in the sun to form a brick. Freshly-mixed brick mixture would be used as mortar when building to 'glue' the bricks together.

A group of workers create mud bricks out of mud, sand, water and straw bought from farmers. All the materials had to be mixed together thoroughly, which was hot, tiring work.

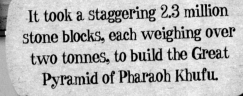

STRIKE!

If you and your colleagues found it all too much, you might be able to strike for better conditions. The world's first known industrial dispute was by building workers at Deir-el-Medina over 3,500 years ago. The workers were successful, getting their delayed payment of grain.

It took a staggering 2.3 million stone blocks, each weighing over two tonnes, to build the Great Pyramid of Pharaoh Khufu.

It's monumental

Some temples, monuments and tombs were built of stone. These could be huge undertakings, involving hundreds or even thousands of workers, who frequently lived in specially-built settlements close to the site. Large stone blocks had to be cut out of quarries and transported to the site. The stone had to be finished off and smoothed to precise dimensions – incredibly tough work for people who were equipped with only hand tools made of copper, stone and bronze. So, there was no going home early or long, lazy lunches for them!

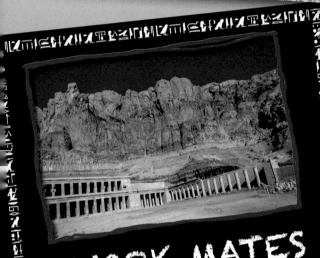

WORK MATES

Architects used their knowledge of rocks and building techniques to plan out constructions before the builders started work. Some advisors to the pharaoh were also important architects such as Imhotep (see page 24) and Senenmut, who is believed to have been the architect of the mortuary temple at Deir-el-Bahari (above).

JOB VERDICT

Not great. Truly back-breaking work for low pay, but for poor men, a big building project gave them a home, food and employment.

VIZIER

Busy body

The vizier was the chief advisor to a pharaoh, a bit like a prime minister but without elections or political parties to worry about. The vizier was appointed by the pharaoh and many were originally scribes at the royal palace. As vizier, you would be busy, busy, busy, handling the affairs of the country. These could range from giving orders to tax collectors and nomarchs (see page 25), appointing officials, ruling on certain crimes, checking on the pharaoh's treasury, farmlands and food supplies and reporting back to the pharaoh regularly.

JOB VACANCY
Start date: 1500 BCE

● ARE YOU CUNNING, SMART AND RUTHLESS?

● CAN YOU WIN ARGUMENTS AND CONVINCE PEOPLE THAT YOUR WAY IS RIGHT?

● ARE YOU GOOD AT MULTITASKING AND MAKING LOTS OF DECISIONS?

Viziers were often in charge of the building of new monuments and in some cases may even have designed them themselves. Imhotep, a vizier to pharaoh Djoser, is believed to have been the architect of the first stepped pyramid, the Djoser pyramid (left) built over 4,600 years ago.

Power and influence

Viziers wore an official outfit which was made up of a long skirt-like piece of clothing knotted around the chest and held in place by two straps. Everyone who was anyone in ancient Egypt knew who the viziers were. They wielded great power and could expect large gifts of land, slaves and gifts in return for their devoted service to the pharoahs. When a pharaoh had no sons and so lacked a direct heir to the throne, a vizier sometimes stepped in temporarily until a new pharaoh was appointed. Some viziers even got the top job themselves – Ramesses I and Amenemhet I were both viziers before they became pharaohs.

Ay or Aya (left) was vizier to the young pharaoh, Tutankhamun, and probably ruled Egypt when the pharaoh was a boy. After Tutankhamun died, Ay officially became pharaoh.

WORK MATES

Ancient Egypt was divided up into 42 regions called nomes. In charge of each was a governor called a nomarch. Most nomarchs inherited the job from their father, but they could be sacked if the pharaoh wasn't pleased with them. Within the nome, the nomarch was responsible for law and order, building projects and collecting taxes.

ODD JOB

FROM HEAD TO TOE

While the vizier was at the head of the pharaoh's staff, others, such as the royal sandal bearer, were literally at the foot. He kept hold of the pharaoh's sandals when they weren't being worn and had to bend low to the ground to put them on the ruler, often kissing the pharaoh's feet before doing so.

JOB VERDICT

Keep on the right side of your pharaoh and being vizier is a great, if rather hectic job. Power, fame, riches and a place in history could all be yours.

METALWORKER

Rock stars

It was often hot in ancient Egypt but some metalworkers dealt with even higher temperatures, heating chunks of rock in large pots on blazing fires to separate out the metal they contained. The molten metal would be poured off and the waste, called slag, thrown away.

Once the metal was recovered, it might be poured into moulds to make certain shapes or hammered flat into blades for weapons or farm implements or into thin sheets for jewellery. Different metals were worked, including some that were imported from other lands, such as copper and tin. The Egyptians later learned how to mix the two together to form bronze.

JOB VACANCY
Start date: 1500 BCE

● CAN YOU HANDLE HEAT, SMOKE AND REALLY BAD SMELLS?

● ARE YOU STRONG ENOUGH TO LIFT HEAVY ROCKS OR CAULDRONS FULL OF METAL?

● DO YOU HAVE GOOD STAMINA SO THAT YOU CAN WORK HARD FOR LONG PERIODS?

ODD JOB

STINKY STORY

In an ancient Egyptian story called 'The teaching of Duaf's son Khety', a wise man explains why metalworking is nowhere near as good a job as being a scribe. He says, "I have seen the metal-worker working at the mouth of his furnace with fingers like the stuff of a crocodile. He stinks more than fish eggs."

A metalworker (top, middle) stokes a fire to get it hotter whilst two men lift a red-hot pot of molten metal.

A crafty career move

Metalworkers had rough, blistered hands and burn scars on their bodies. Their lungs were damaged by all the toxic smoke and fumes they breathed in as they went about their work. Better working conditions were enjoyed by people who crafted jewellery, fine ornaments and luxury objects out of metals such as gold, silver and electrum (an alloy of gold and silver). However, even a craftworker's job could be tough. Craftworkers spent long hours bent over their bench, doing the painstaking work required to produce delicate and intricate objects without modern tools to help them.

Fit for a queen, Queen Ahhotep to be precise, this gold bracelet is inset with a semi-precious blue stone called lapis lazuli.

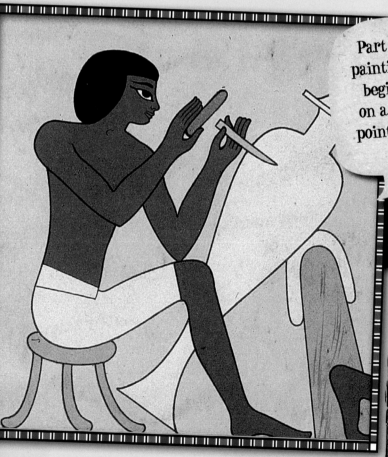

Part of an ancient Egyptian painting shows a craft worker beginning to etch a pattern on a large silver vase using a pointed metal punch struck by a small stone.

JOB VERDICT

Pretty harsh, unless you managed to gain a reputation for excellent craftwork or rose to become a supervisor and oversaw others doing all the unpleasant work.

MUSICIANS, DANCERS AND ACROBATS

Party on!

Wealthy Egyptians liked nothing more than a party. These entertainments created employment for a number of people, including full-time make-up artists and dancers but especially for musicians. Ancient Egyptian musicians played instruments including the lute, harp, lyre, flute and the sistrum – a percussion instrument with metal loops that made a jangling sound when it was shaken. Sometimes, musicians played a double flute – two flutes at the same time, although sadly this didn't result in double pay.

JOB VACANCY
Start date: 1500 BCE

- CAN YOU PLAY A LYRE, A FLUTE OR A HARP?
- DO YOU LIKE PARTIES AND PERFORMING TO BIG CROWDS?
- ARE YOU PREPARED TO PRACTISE TO BECOME A TOP MUSICIAN?

Two musicians play the harp (left) and the lute. The ancient Egyptian harp was either triangular or a long curved shape. The lute featured a small wooden box and long wooden neck. Fitted with two, three or four strings, it was played in a similar way to a modern guitar.

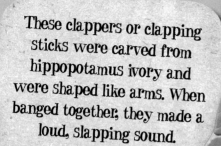

These clappers or clapping sticks were carved from hippopotamus ivory and were shaped like arms. When banged together, they made a loud, slapping sound.

Top job

One of the best jobs for a musician was to become a shemayet – a musician at a temple. This high-status post was often held by women who, as well as playing at the temple, provided music at religious festivals and sometimes even in the fields during harvest time. Musicians who were hired to play at private feasts and parties did not enjoy such high status, but some earned a good living and were given free food.

ODD JOB

SCENTED WAX

Servants at a party were entrusted with the task of placing wax cones of sweet-smelling incense on the heads of guests! The cone would melt during the evening and helped mask the pong of lots of people crammed together at a party or banquet.

WORK MATES

Dancers were hired for many parties as well as religious ceremonies. The dancers might be male or female, but mixed groups never performed together. Dances were often planned carefully in advance and some involved acrobatics. Dancers wore very little clothing and sometimes fixed bells around their waist which sounded as they moved.

JOB VERDICT

Not bad at all if you get enough bookings. You get to show off your skills in front of happy partygoers but may have to busk in public or do other jobs to make ends meet.

QUIZ

Which job in ancient Egypt would you be most suited to? Answer the questions below then turn the book upside down to read the verdict!

Questions

1 **Are you good with gore?**

a) Yup. Blood and guts don't bother me.

b) I'm not too bad with a bit of blood.

c) Urgh! No way.

2 **Do you like physical activity and being outside?**

a) I don't mind a gentle walk outside and I like plants and flowers.

b) Yes, I am fit and love working up a sweat in the great outdoors.

c) No, I prefer staying inside and reading.

3 **Are you ambitious and do you like being in charge?**

a) I don't mind some responsibility but don't need to be in charge.

b) Too much like hard work! I'd rather be told what to do.

c) I prefer to be in charge and have no problems telling others what to do.

4 **Are you patient and good with your hands?**

a) I am fairly patient and reasonably good with my hands.

b) No, not very. I much prefer to charge in and get things done.

c) Yes, I am good with fiddly things and have bags of patience.

Answers

Mostly As
You might make a good embalmer or doctor in ancient Egypt.

Mostly Bs
A soldier's life is a possibility for you, as is being an ancient Egyptian builder.

Mostly Cs
A scribe might be your ideal line of work, or possibly being a priest or an architect.

Glossary

amulets Lucky charms worn by ancient Egyptians.

censuses Counts of how many people live in a country carried out by officials from the government.

corvee A form of tax paid by ancient Egyptians by giving their time and labour to work on building projects.

drift net A type of fishing net that hangs from fishing boats into the water.

embalmer A person who prepares dead bodies to preserve them before burial.

hieratic A type of writing script, simpler than hieroglyphs, used in ancient Egypt.

hieroglyphic A system of writing using symbols and pictures.

industrial dispute A disagreement between workers and the people they work for over pay or conditions.

irrigation Channelling water from a river or stream to farmland.

natron A type of salt used to preserve bodies during mummy-making.

nomarch A governor or local ruler of a Nome, a district in ancient Egypt.

ostraca Pieces of broken pottery on which trainee scribes might practise their writing.

papyrus A type of reed used to make boats, baskets and paper-like sheets.

pharaoh The ruler of ancient Egypt.

sickle A farm tool with a long curved blade for cutting crops such as wheat.

vizier The pharaoh's chief advisor.

Further Information

Books

The History Detective Investigates: Ancient Egypt – Rachel Minay (Wayland, 2014)

At Home With The Ancient Egyptians – Tim Cooke (Wayland, 2014)

Mangy Mummies, Menacing Pharaohs and Awful Afterlife – Kay Barnham and Tom Morgan-Jones (Wayland, 2014)

Websites

http://www.pbs.org/empires/egypt/newkingdom/pharaohs.html
and
http://www.pbs.org/wgbh/nova/ancient/explore-ancient-egypt.html
Learn about a number of famous pharaohs and enjoy some extraordinary views of the amazing structures of ancient Egypt at these Public Broadcasting Service web pages.

http://www.ancientegypt.co.uk/trade/home.html
Explore two ancient Egyptian workshops at this site brought to you by the British Museum.

http://www.childrensuniversity.manchester.ac.uk/interactives/history/egypt
Find out about the lives of ancient Egyptians at the Children's University of Manchester.

http://www.nms.ac.uk/explore/play/discover-ancient-egypt
Learn about ancient Egyptian tombs at this National Museum of Scotland website.

INDEX